OPERATIONS OF WATER

IAN SEED

KFS

Newton-le-Willows

Published in the United Kingdom in 2020
by The Knives Forks And Spoons Press,
51 Pipit Avenue,
Newton-le-Willows,
Merseyside,
WA12 9RG.

ISBN 978-1-912211-66-1

Acknowledgements:

Some of these poems first appeared in the following publications: *An Educated Desire* (a Knives, Forks and Spoons anthology in tribute to Robert Sheppard), *Black Box Manifold*, *Fidelities* (a Red Ceilings chapbook, 2015) *Great Works*, *Long Poem Magazine*, *Matter*, *Molly Bloom*, *Poetry Salzburg Review*, *Shearsman*, and *Stride*.

LOTTERY FUNDED
Supported using public funding by
ARTS COUNCIL ENGLAND

'My hat's as wet as back then in Paris'

—Kurt Schwitters

Contents

1

2

3

4

1

Ziggurat

1

We love the rolling broadleaf
of your anatomy. Let's hope

the rental suntanned strangers
at a loose end occur

about this silent, new white sofa.
Across the world, wider girls

skipped our sleeve. I had a teacher
knowing it was mine,

gets his first man-bun,
but it's when you see

people start blasting,
I gotta show you the sea.

I want to have it personal
so we can share a nifty coda.

2

You know the feeling
with you right next to me

to put it politely
wolfing the cheeky.

That's the good news.
Let's talk a dark wood

leather bound aesthetic.
There's no better metaphor.

If only I could get to you
before the geese

balance right together,
remote from the sense of sinking

or floating the curve
and dip wander behind them.

3

Their sausages are made from serious.
Their teeth are especially brittle

moneyed light. You need
only clock the punters

salted and sticky mount up.
I mean I have an excuse

render and crisped.
Everything is lubricated.

It feels like good
and subsequent employment

my lips have kissed.
My dad stayed and was, like,

the elephant above Blake's cot
and the can of knotted.

4

Liquid elsewhere items ramp.
Quite a few high street

bits the breath out of me.
Take the pill to your face

and front engine. It's still
quite hinge and bottom

through which Gaspard
the donkey is cannoned.

He has invalided out
enormous guests. Seems like a lark

and a group of apple trees
pimped with my cousin

in a fragrant casket, pink
plump in the empty part.

5

We picked and lost a lovely
pair. Here is the well

familiar barmaid *tête de veau*
was cattle grazing

those big-eyed chewers.
It wasn't his hand, so why

do we do the things we do
black on white? The shape

of your name
I hope is not a sign

you're offloading. You have a choice,
your space quite brims.

I was invited to its screwing
last week. Unbelievable.

6

How did you and Gaspard meet?
My family itself were the tools

Brexit. My wife can shrink
a French horn, I may add

oversized birds that our father
stitched himself poo head gesturing

so easily one lowers into the ruins
headgear plastic clear streams.

We can expect the cracks
hogged off down the road

their destination plural kissing
decades of bums. There's this duality.

We are the active 86%, and it's not only sweaty.
We found a kind of church in it, you monkey.

7

It all adds up, that's the piercing
something of a bumper

franchise if you really want
to amp up the romance.

Spidery is the spark of youth
jostling up a buck backlit,

a good song though not high enough
to look into its face. The sand

coloured chap is as limp
as a dead bird. That's a ziggurat

teetering, and not half
so intimate. We picked at our stump.

It is, hands down,
your first task to mix a cocktail.

Domestic

The plate got up and walked across the table
There was some fun in your eye
Spite of the no-nonsense no-how look
It seems I have been planning the tone
Born of a four-legged desire
I agreed to come to an agreement
Find the wanton thee by the roadside
It's all one to me I should say so
Bringing it up on the bright bus
It's all one with this wilderness
First it was the only one to marry me
I know who kept it so easily and young
While it was worth waiting for
Not down by the worst river but other
One side took it and then the none
For me to come to you this way
Is another story altogether
Come to us via a tear duct
Or perhaps a million of them
This head brought on a plate
No telling whose path this is
Once in a while we keep to it
Flying into the intimate space of you
Not crying out loud perhaps
Yet down the whitening heal of your cut
The distance dubbed over with unfinished rain

Landing

The shell sits in sunlight, your new flirt buddy.
There is much talk of 'our mother'. It is true
that the pink scar a child never quite loved
was the badge of thousands of fish.

What's your real name? Someone
has told the bouncers to be nice. If I could speak
I could show you who I really am, engaged
with the holes in the side of a film strip

of snaps along the sands to the dunes.
Why aren't you at home? We won't make you
think for yourself. It's a free ride to the sky, pretty one
where she pours her curves, but I take you

to a smaller landing, where I'm always hanging about.
Some bum notes. We're nice boys,
have been going strong down the passage
with little sign of disintegrating, holding

our wet hands to our mouths, despite being made
of rubber with visible bolts and junctions
up the rotten stairs, remaking our city.
There are 'good girls' and 'bed girls'

loved and died the day I was sentenced
still heavy from a dream because they cannot keep
a secret. They wear masks, too. Just do the maths.
Eat six Weetabix for breakfast. Nothing but dirty white

comes down into my arms, ripped open at the knees.
We'll just have to wipe everything off here, for I shan't sleep.
You need me to do something to you, a random weave.
Hear her apologising down the corridor. There, just take hold of this.

Making up John and Jane and having them do things
her questing tongue would translate. Carry on, sergeant.
I went out of the hotel into the snow, flecked with black.
There's something funny going to happen. It's about to begin.

Ground Rules

The breeze radiates and sparkles and cannot be grasped.
You are in the middle, your tunic freshly washed,
like a messenger about to be sent on a royal mission.
But once on the path you reach a solitude that is not
in your control and cannot be sweetened

by the nerve doctor who emerges naked from behind
his door. You find you have learnt a lot of his books
by heart unintentionally, especially the beginnings
of paragraphs. He shows you real things, drills you
and gives you an overcoat with a different plot to it,

more than mere protection against cold air. But that puzzled
manner he has of peering often changes to a shrewd
and thrusting glance, the end of his road plain before him.
When two little brooks come together they make a real run
he says, blocking your way. He believes in you as a bridge

between two states of being. He cannot clasp enough shadows
and dust. It is terrible the way he nuzzles you
and makes you lonelier still. In the end you are forced to fight
like a barefooted urchin scrambling for an unexpected prize.
Although you look much the same when you emerge,

things unknown have a secret influence, such as great gasps
of river air at night. Laying down your life takes on a new phase
of meaning. You have no impulse towards death but you understand it
now as if light were turned on a picture and what
you see is worse than featureless dark. The accident

of sex has made you remote and the signature
of your thesis is the basis of a duality as absolute
as an empty, clean-swept house, the nearest
to an authentic message you have come across.
Now your awkward body can move on, no longer

the external creature known to the world. Yet there seems to be
no way of escape, no opening into the professions or what
might be termed Progress Street. An old dog for once
stirs from the kitchen fireside to bark in your wake.
At night you light candles until your eyes shine.

Lukewarm after a Wet Dream

We read the distance, passage it to optic nerves
the blind man knows, though to this extent
it is put into the mouth, brought into play

as a mere equation. The funnel places its lips
for in fog or smoke from which nothing emerges,
we may speak and give the mouth a name,

a vanishing place, but now we go, colours blurry
and everything else is white paper, open
like an abandoned house, in which we move about,

only to convene in the fragile rain. Likewise
some others are there – the wheel turns as it is turned,
the black and white points of view of people

who walk around the rooms become each other's
backgrounds. If they run away, all is lost
for there in the sky the dangers of lightning touch the forehead.

The dark woman waiting so long will be upheld. I am on my way,
one sunny step further. Take care that the door opens
perfect breasts bared on the orders of the one who rests

more sweetly. There he is in the bar again. I have given
this dream in full with curved edges. As we turn our heads,
the woman with closed eyes and unknown sleep accepts the dark as her own.

Certain Nakednesses

1

Finely hairy below large lobe-like teeth
I was converted in my own bedroom in my father's rectory
from unseasoned wood

Small oval pods split to release fluffy seeds
Hollow elm trunks suckered freely
Only then was I allowed to proceed

We must class him with these fruits' good bearing
pendulous side shoots, netlike veins on the membranous wings
in waves of liquid love the best wooden wheelbarrows

most beautiful in early summer, like the very breath
deeply-toothed, sparsely hairy leaves larger more heart-shaped
stems encased in raggedy fuzzily imparted clues

2

You must not leave me till I understand
the wild wood in which the inner man rolls over crown open
sweeping besoms of birch twigs grey and smooth then brown with pink fissures

Little-branched, I fear to lose the truth
knowing an officer on our force lasts and saddles trees
This intercourse is realised at the time as being both active and mutual

Early settlers arrive by boat ending in a notch
Bright red bark like a bed is pushed up
against a common city window

the unpleasant smell opening and grinds
more curved horns and a small raised bump
had been lifted into a position for which I was too small

3

His foot was on a kind of lightening drooping foliage
It was his pathway ripened black through winter
That is why there is a smile upon the face

The branding flame stalks the dark
glossy curly leaves of the male trees
One day his friend met him in the rain, a fine cigar

and a cloud of smoke setting fruits in globular clusters
purple-black, bitter-tasting, those unnecessary trimmings
of lace, ribbons and buttons, dense heads of small white flowers

In these journeys I have been where much cloth has been dyed
lobes less deeply cut when stained
washing our garments to keep them sweet

Varieties

after William James

The naked bill of fare – in it the inner man rolls over.
When I come to try, I find I cannot. The hands and feet
on these terms are in a different position entirely, as though
the name were jammed between hills and valley.

Have you got your psalter with you? Never be cornered. What shape
by multiplying clothes shall you make your body. He may make his bed.
Down this shape my intelligence glided paths on which one ought
not to wander. I must speak more fully soon.

A day stripped, therefore in our rooms I got up to dress myself
so staringly bare, making the one move out of his mouth. He took
his text *et la mal dans ma bouche*, where these things haunt, where the bones are
passed unhappy quarters, the me, the we. It made his back

put them on at night, or shrink away. There is a verge of the mind.
I can do nothing the nights in winter never so long
I have strung scattered passages together, but only colours
you cease to open yourself a few faces among rows of empty chairs

alone on the seashore along this path the giggly bubbly filmiest of screens.
It is only the first step that costs the creepy rich bloke the factors of some dream.
'God is very good,' he said, but if you have nothing else there's the return
to a sort of half-sleep. The trick succeeds –

who got the sergeant's job? Walk about a lot for no apparent reason,
but on the cleanest, the surest of streets, a wave
going through me follows it along. It seems like the very breath.
Falling rocks? Gull attacks? The downward ladder? I shall die if these waves continue.

They all seem to be in underwear. When I walked the fields,
it was like entering another world. It remains so essentially
unbroken everything is new. The addition of such a sense
presses forward towards the village. The people, the fields, the cattle, the trees

(they all seem to be in underwear) stop going to church. The appearance
of everything has a deeper voice, a dirt mark. The work is finished.
Pathfinders transparent, an entirely black dog keeps some sense
of fluidity, the whole day turning before me, the rich thicket

up and down the streets of the town. I find myself there alone
while my first self weeps. You believe as little as I do, coming out of the café.
Another filled his glass. Most of them in their turn, jammed as it were,
have remained empty. That was the idea.

2

Danger in the Water

Consider yourself boarding a ship. The sailors' tune lingers on the last note
as if lying in wait. Our faces show the colour of our hearts. The water
flows crystal-clear down the middle of the street. It cannot
fail for a river is a rite, though it resembles a figure

so strange, now jumping close. To be in the living water,
no longer hold it against us, stiff and cold! You cannot fail to reach
through the empty window into the little harbour, as we stand
on the banks in a fair life, empty cans and bottles bobbing in the foam.

Oh you along the way, you really don't know anything. The little fish
receiving the water meets our guide. I come from inland, too.
A current under here breaks off the owner of the bark, I alone
with open face. I'll puff him through the porthole into the waves,

winning back our connection with the wind. I'll run on and be glad
of manufactured dreams through all the open fields. We have returned.
The flat world has become high, deep and wide. Still in nightshirts,
we'll rush so swiftly towards the royal stream, and those smaller chambers.

Thus once I saw the footmen so familiar yet thought I had forgotten them.
I want to seek out quantities of those little creatures, their brilliance
to open us. Listen to the argument that is in my heart. Push them gently
back into the water, every tongue trembling under a wayward sun.

Milestone

We arrive at the end of our voyage on the road's watery surface,
at the top of the sharp rising, hands deep in coat pockets.
Let's lean for a moment against the stone wall. I'm an adult
but I'm very young, and feel like saying 'Mr' by a sudden

turning of the road. Bridges are only too well known. The
September breeze bangs at the door. It's difficult to call you
by your first name, though I mark well the cold slashes
of the roofs on the horizon. Somehow they reconnect me.

You are my elder, myself unseen. The only glimmer
is to know what it is to be born, to be led on step by step
and have visits from buddies. Can you get me out of here?
Science, technology, physical activity. You are more than welcome

unless you come clothed in military garb, and with all
the latest tales. I could have taken a different route, but I leave
the station with an unknown companion, still looking toward the village.
All are gone to rest. It's death on the river when we cast back

into the past. What will happen to us? First, eat, but how?
Clearly and colourfully, it's the language of these people
in this city. There's a strange half-absence, aside from the concierge's
daughter, sometimes fuzzy. I am separated from her by the crowd

at the door I knocked on only a few moments ago. A two-room
rental flat with your own furniture and a good few years to remember.
Squeezed, touched indifferently on all sides, I still linger by the door
but I keep my trap shut. The memoirist is of course making it up.

I think of both of them. I am afraid for them. A little space –
the vast bordello of the capital, a language spoken decades earlier.
My home is hidden away somewhere. Will I find it again?
Excuse me just a moment – a shot of whiskey will make me

less afraid. She prays in her own language while I telephone,
trembling like all good fellows of my calling, with some flicker
of grace. With my back to the wall, I call after her
on the other side, ready now once more, pants down.

Preparations

Guide water to their fields, or put on other garments.
It's quite a long way back to shape our lives
or carry forth the ashes. You have to contort
your face a bit, yet these are true – take a handful.

Swift and spirited, this is the offering, but not
to the sky, nor the ocean to which the living
have returned. Their wings or fins are joined
to one another, their costumes are on fire.

Some reach the other shore. A highway
shall be there, and another. Moved by the wind,
who can be warm alone? Then I returned
and perceived their vanity. Choose the path

of preparations of the heart. It is steep
in history. There is an island, a farther shore
to call passengers who go right on their ways.
It seems to die away, apart from our perceiving

on the lips of him. You can see inside the house
which has been abandoned. You do not need to search
for a door. Among the simple ones, I see you
before me. Do you remember what I wrote

on the wall by the window frame? The first word
begins here. The second begins invisible
and subtle of heart. You did the right thing –
the motion of a sling, the fall of a stone,

catches and kisses him. Oh, the small cities,
the technique of 'dirty sound'. I have decked my bed
at the Cafe Vasco. These are of two kinds.
By means of their operations, I am not at home,

I have gone a long journey. Wish me a good morning
with a word of love. It tears truths from the straitjacket,
draws me out of many waters. I have heard your footsteps
calm and slow where the mirror is the surface.

Keep me as the apple of your eye. How beautiful you are,
engaged in faithfulness. The mouth is full
with no time to wait. It's a theory of love although we
turn from him. There are people who note everything

which happens in the city. They were spread abroad.
You may think you will never, but out of the loss
comes sweetness. You feel strangely drawn away.
Everything is in order, and runs. What used to pass

for a thick covering of hair is thinning out, wounded
on the stones of wandering lanes. The universe vanishes.
The heave shoulder and the wave show up their crisp handling.
Things have neither voice nor colour, nor confide anything in us.

Church Steps

They jump because the girls I know have a 'g'
for gorgeous, though I have nothing for them to drink.
Permettez-moi un mot sale. Here the nouns linger,
sure to be a treat, yet the hinges of the man

who steadies the ladder refuse to connect. He has knees,
maybe white eyes with peeling skin. I have nothing
to fill out the sails of this sleety day, which washes us
through a larger passage of a forgotten history.

I have employed a man who will not leave, who carries
a death wish inside him. *Voila, votre mort,*
Monsieur, is not lost from a tiny hole in the ceiling.
I have been out. I have seen how relative absence

descends a long see-through tube. It hankers after
the little plumber who can arrange everything. It's sure
to be a treat. Coiled, polished, we can make the leap.
How small I must have been before my body

became a stranger to itself. It's something of a joke:
the man steadies his ladder, puts up a poster
of a naked figure. We are baptised in puddle water
by the church steps. If only I could slake my thirst.

Phantom Limbs

After Maurice Merleau-Ponty

Clouds wander like thinkers in midair, only
to reassemble, remote on the horizon. Our flesh
takes its place among arrangements of fields,
their colours and smells formed in our hearts.

We do not see from our bodies as from inside
a box. We pertain to the whole, we take our place
in the landscape, in the touching of the sleek and rough.
A finger on the rim of a glass makes a ring

reverberate in the air. At a certain time you recall
another time on another day. This will always
be true. We move towards a thing of which
in the end there is nothing to say. This wave

rises within us between the touched and the touching.
If we break a stone, we can feel its pieces, but once
a picture is torn, it no longer exists. Yet if I look
or remember long enough, a constellation emerges,

pregnant with texture. Though it will change or disappear,
its fragments remain to touch lightly. No need
to make believe. Understanding comes from lingering
on the edge of these fields. Emptiness is not nothing.

Greetings

His face meets mine on the shore, with its freeze
furled in a dream of a lake. He asks me
who I am. A child enters by a secret door,
light as a fable, no longer wearing his coat.

A world has gone from his eyes. I picture
the house from outside, its stones the colour
of time. Ghosts are for the living. They nestle
and warm us at the stem. Nothing so still

as he who moves the past around in pictures
though it keeps running away. When we move
our eyes, the view changes: the distance comes
closer. The landscape and our wandering gaze

are glued together in the upsurge of a true
and exact world. Your finger plays across
its surface, pointing to a tree on the far side.
Leafless, motionless, it might be dead or alive.

And here's the slope going down to the water,
where an empty boat trapped in the ice awaits
with wordless logic. By the tree whose roots
are drowning, your hand stretches out to help me in.

Fidelities

The dark thing that lies upstairs takes
nothing for granted. It remains faithful
in a world of deserters, plotters and perpetual
beginners. Its footnotes alone have validity

at the bottom of a narrative coloured with fire.
The sun grows as it goes down. See that redhead?
I lace my shoes and cross the road, a stranger
but not of foreign blood. Is it okay to share

your toothbrush? Or to wear your pyjamas?
My dreams wander around the distant town.
One path makes me think of another where
flowers crowd or fall about you. Faces

vanish down the street. Some coatless exile
descends at the end of a station platform. The charms
of roaming through smoke where memory dirties
its own threads! In this clump of survivors,

we sift through pieces of each other's dreams,
fluctuating life stories to be shared, you
in his room on the bed, fast and slippery and wet,
a dark space between the real and not-real.

Once True

There is always the risk
you might give birth, so hold
what is, but do not hold it
to be anything. Be careful
not to think too long
at the bottom of the river
without light. So far
nothing real. You are
swallowed. I remember
the night and almost
the spot on the hillside,
the instance of the moon
given up. I see you
have wandered at your own
sweet will. You remain
enclosed in the midst of
everything. I have had
such trouble meeting you,
who once passed so
laughingly by, now
entangled with a heart
in coils, seeking to recall
the change in colours
when the breeze dropped.
In the summer there was
nothing easier than to
gather flowers. Each

morning you would go
like one on the true path,
and later like a doll
you bent over the side
of a tiny boat, your fingertips
dipping into the water. There
was always a lovelier one
you could not reach.

Ian Seed

From a Small Notebook

The means of return still shines from the page –
with a cold thin breath, I am plunging in. It can only deepen
like a final judgement from a distance
where the ridge goes out.
Two souls lean against each other – we know nothing,
we move about like shades, tears down our backs,
not knowing who he is, or you, *donna gentile*
in the steep cut gorge. All the peaks
are covered with snow – why is this one bare?
He spreads out his fingers on the young grass,

before departing explores his brow.
Here is the old man in search of something
still unknown. An angel comes. His wings spread wide
better waters. As if awakened I admit that I do not know.
I find myself forgiven
when I return to where we were staying.
She opens the door for me, but the funeral slabs
on the church floor are caked with ice.
She is smiling, inching along in the midst of these.
She twists her face beneath her burden.

I do not learn whose voice this is.
Knees are joined to breasts. A frozen lake. The door
grinds at its hinges. Feet crackle on ice.
How can an angel be unreal?
I can tell you better over by the well.

Inside, voices sing, but not only of his body.
That sticky warm smell of her I know
but indistinctly. The two figures huddle on the floor,
ripple in a single flame, its many hands alive
while songs of the dead float over.

Burst

'a face that paints its human evasions' – Robert Sheppard

in pictures of the city
you unconceal
the shape of space
between figures

a whisper moves
along a wire
stretching back
a sky unhazed

nothing yet
in the counterbeat
testimony of air
but here dreams

are given a voice
by the silence
in the room of a poem
now painting rain

across heaven
its lines grey
or loose black
down from the page

Whisper

The self becomes a husk when,
with fragments of glass, we paint
the wounds of our ancestors.

The accretions of myth are stripped
away so that finally we are even less
ourselves. Ghosts follow us

in the syntax of our dance, yet in no way
resemble it, their footsteps without resonance
as if to atone both for their leaving

and their return. They take my words
as if I were the narrator of only one story
never fully real. I've had it

up to my eyebrows with drawing
the dead. Your lips have a plan
of escape, still faintly palpable.

Beach

Unnamed, this city by the sea ended up as my home.
I found my feet renting out deckchairs, scanning for silver.

There are no landmarks to navigate by, but keep an eye out
for glints in the sand. The further you go, the emptier it gets.

Beautiful as it is here, it can get quite windy, and it may happen to rain.
Better the distance as the crow flies. Let things be what they are

or nab one of the grassy knolls without messing up its delicate neural map.
The rabbit burrows into the hill of the spirits. Kelly's ice cream van

sometimes drops by in misleading versions of itself.
It does not look for things, but there's good rock pooling here.

You can see slices of time in the water. You can catch
the curve of ripples in a template and a bird flying overhead

leaves its reflection, though the waves are much steeper
back on the main beach with our left-over bits

swept up and bound away. After a while they're all
the same, like houses in a street. You can't remember

the one you were waiting for. If only I could slip my hands
into Mr Punch. He is more than just a silly voice.

3

Absences

1

Years pass in the little room
in the harbour town. The sea sparkles
but you no longer feel the power

beneath its colours. You never speak
to the sad girl across the hallway.
Towards evening, the hillside

turns black, the streets are emptied
and the sea grows still. Each morning
you search the traces of your dreams

for a story, but they are no more
than flat, unconnected pictures
made by a child's crayons.

2

Just outside the broken window
where a spider hangs, waves
drag pebbles. From somewhere

in the night, there's a rich
throaty singing. The breathing
of the sleepers on the floor

makes me lonelier still.
I can hardly make out the face
next to mine, just a blade of light

in the eyes. Don't wake the others,
she whispers. Her lips taste
of wine and smoke and sea.

3

The small happy boy in the photo
is now the unstable man who
crosses the road to the station.

All the pieces of the early landscape
have been lost without powder
or smoke in the interstices

of a dream where we grow
unbroken. Your friend would
understand, wouldn't she? But not

the part that is dead and frozen
in a hotel room with a stranger
with little stars sewn into his eyes.

4

I wait outside. He will not tolerate
intruders. A smile is slashed
across his face in the window.

Each heart will stop beating.
There's terror in the simplest act,
such as crossing an empty street.

Once we ran through fields
with the taste of sun. Now when you speak
or look at me, I turn

to the distance inside my head
as if someone else were waiting there
in a window in another story.

5

The shape of your mouth
produces its own truth,
unlike the weightiness

of your conclusions.
You talk as if your life
were that of another,

each embrace
a marginal event
instead of an alchemy

of blood in a dark
warm place hidden
behind the heart.

6

Your face is turned away
in the half light. I do not know
if you are starting to cry.

The empty window is black.
It challenges me to touch it
and enter, as if it were a dark sea

with all the secrets of a life.
You are falling, as if being born,
yet the light you emerge into

is nothing else *but* light, as if
you had gone straight into death
with no living or dying inbetween.

7

In this incompleteness, I make up
my own story, begin over
and over again without ever

entering the plot, hanging on
to the privilege of not knowing.
Where the window is scratched

is a greyness like an echo
of where I've never been.
To be far away without

knowing it, to lose yourself,
to become alive in a country
with a blue, unbroken sky…

8

You must have mistaken me
for someone else. I want good news,
not the feeling of sadness

brought by photos in out-of-date
magazines in waiting rooms. I have
a friend who says that all journeys

by definition are broken. The path
loses itself in the trees. Faces
fade, so that in the end you have to

invent new ones, made up
of bits and pieces of those you knew
and loved, or couldn't, before.

9

Because of the umbrella, I couldn't see
her face. We crossed the square
to the station. 'Find a job and place

to live – I'll join you.' An unreal
world achieves its own consistency.
You look out of the window

at the train on the next platform
and for a moment you think
you're moving. A breath of wind

passes and never returns. Often
in the midst of things, I close my
eyes and dream I'm falling.

10

You told me your dream
without understanding any
of the figures who moved through,

whose progress was measured
in fingers of random rain.
The dead stay caught

listening to those they love.
Under the bridge, she ended up
knowing so much, like how

to become imperceptible. What then
is true mourning? The voyage
turns out to be a return.

11

In what sense are our sensations
private? We argued over who
had got the better kiss. The story

was simple: how we slipped
into different company and beds,
as if tied into an old tale

of a search for shining gold,
which, however faraway, assumed
the shape of the moment.

The silent road stretching
into the distance is happy
without our footsteps.

12

We waited in the station all night.
When I lit your cigarette, your hand
trembled around the flame,

which made its own brief country
on your face. The distance from
eyes to lips forms its own

neighbourhood. I was back where
I started, between two worlds. At the border
they asked endless questions.

They led me into another room
while I tried to remember your name,
pressed against something invisible.

13

Shadows are broken by patches
of light. Known for their silences
these ghosts you dream of

are not able to enter the landscape
though each brings a fresh eye.
You have the impression that he still

looks at you the way he first did
when you sat by a train window
pretending not to notice, tinkering

with a cigarette. If you knock there
along the bones from the past, smoke
will tell its own story passing through.

Vacation

More and more we think of what might have been,
though we put on a show of carrying on.
It takes finding to show what it was
we were looking for. How blue the sky seems

once we've got a clear picture. If I could run
towards it, take hold of it. In patterns
recurring, the old times bring their worn lines
and figures. The sun rapidly darkens.

Its rise too was speedy. Hang on in there,
story. Between the opening and closing
there are still episodes to be discovered,
not yet consigned to a back number

where the print is smaller and greyer.
Now we've arrived, I wish to make friends
with the little town, in the places where
it isn't faded, where the sun is just so.

Shift

While I write by the window, such
ghosts watch the house, consider
the emerging shape of a youth
in front of a mirror, a face

from shave to shave unfolding.
Its *is* is different each day,
but always the same revenant
wanders in, holding a lamp.

'The sun was never brighter,' he says,
'and this apparatus is its gaze.
Here is the past, which starts
in the present. With backwards logic

its questions may leave you
no lessons as you move the pen
across the page, a dancer
discovering each step as it's taken.'

Vein

We enjoy the fiction of encounters, their meaning
in the margins, yet growing from there to be
so true they become everything without us
realising. Ten minutes have passed and we

are nowhere, our feet not touching the ground,
the future as someone else's life. There are those
we have never outgrown. We wish them well.
Everyone must wait to come out of their own tale.

I open my father's copy. It tells the truth
of his life on a great steam train in an ancient
colouring book, its lines traced finely through
my heart, yet lent weight by their scarcity.

Why, lad, are you here? Because sometimes
that's all there is. At the end of the station platform,
coatless exiles share fluctuating life stories,
their white shirts deleted or flickering in the steam.

Plot

In an age of oval-shaped romance pictures,
dumb letters as downloads, should we scrap it all
for 'authentic' writing, like a bloody cleft
washed by the waves, which carry torn up

messages away in the fringe of their flood?
Who is playing whom in this deathless sketch
of an old master, where a woman with a deep
red scarf deftly skirts a man who remains

alone in a breathless stance before an all-
too-familiar shaving mirror? We may watch
in the belief that each movement makes
for a whole. We may guess and grasp at codes.

But in a stripping of bodies, how can you tell
from a lit-up window which one is yours? You can't
put your finger on them. The story has to begin again
with its tale of a figure never quite centred in its frame.

4

Operations of Water

1

its colourless mouth has shaped unseizable words

you in yourself circle where you still my arms to return ready-made

without boundaries it gives a lake a last clean

takes on shadow substance but the place already and again opening its tender

bearing tears of cold childhood directions all fluid impossible

and night transparent your skeleton clothes has skin arrived

and always another inside you I wanted fluids lips could instrument

the pulse of petals in their suspended unfolding

and vertical again only no longer touching remain open

I and together unfrozen of eyes have wandered near mouths

the hidden it under your door I the answered opening on melt

and fingers gentle the clean cry my small body facedown

2

a snow inside mist on you undresses a bare spread floor

that his voice doesn't hang fingers with song between growing

ice only move in departing the next body explores at first his inching

warm tiny life brow having midst at this still means search

huddled together in the returning face tears shine beneath one streaming

from unknown and his bundle down the angels burden

we bowed its page and learn cold whose journeys voice this centre deepen

long seems song itself where it hits the light leans

little distance know his will begins arms forgive in valley

wings where spread the form the wide him floor and that ridge

as of peering out something rippling promises again each safe

as a single secret to its exercise a breast a hands hammer

3

known frozen are in nothing more alive if the one hand about stars

like glass touches chief shades of ourselves fluid forgotten

the floating dark they shape steep where will and cut sound not a gorge of open

in walking emerge among outspread patterns on into the ice one cedars

entering the designs its grass tells seams wandering path over angels new

covered they are by day no longer to light resembles

streaming in of birds and ice catching large around the labyrinth but long was kissed

letter home the new unwinding paths us to light it

sparkles pause beyond any and to the mouth return

in a rotund somewhere the end dark haired for stranger

dressed from behind the journey sea eye beaten without

a gleam never dissolved a brightly used boundary footsteps code

4

skin listening outside an open zero story bridge unsteady

made of rubble sand water for faith the in beyond

big toothed the possible whiteness my eyed dark

elsewhere a fill bone slowly deep the butterfly such that flocks

a thing even exists of release already broken

his afterwards all heart gridlines each stream

a kiss to break veined wire never more the perceived stranger

the sea keep my end that the sleeve of his feeling

scent opens colour however encircles straightaway

were landscape as spread of this wave is severing sleek rises

in abyss and within depth we the rough concretions

are afferent always nerves a sole understanding phantom

5

in emerge say and the dresses two the tangible sides

gathering body a human of that in gap holds

sway the curved mirror as corpse beings

appear one broken wafer thin night are my

belly who jostle friends now I help unpack begin

the traveller open will end masks still blow may

for worn everyone has and fold design of dead

as it clothes go moment and are naked over like machine

only otherwise leaving lanes to think between skyline hung

bridges prove rivers say his friendly voice and down

us never figure the toss reached careless what clothes almost

decent once more the cry enters itself which hope

6

in a wide dose rivers left to grow were down their rapidly web

counted in night I stroll untouched threads forest dreamt

the made stage of matter sing back have the deeper wear

as almost parts a child done no dark sailors running

footprints red in a want love handkerchief

could knot to street you through the made in one move

the magic printing with the time leap as all tall

from far milk houses one is miracles already

skin unknown dark to their whiter another debt

sometimes up daylight those things tip the touched

cupped heart that a leaf in a moment loosens the lost faces

and the going pointed star to night us is still there

7

separated young with all are only and feel linger

by the latest road bridges the cold slashes of grace

with sometimes fuzzy afraid by the wall still making

visits your own language your coat pocketed on the prays

and breeze bangs as we stand manufactured dreams through

the royal street cannot fail forgotten the last note as if lying under hold

resembles a lake is a river in my heart push so strangers

once I saw them gently toward sun stream through

the evening unheld morning you of singing never harbour

waves drag room in rich more than blade ever the light

power hangs emptied and out a hillside more than wake waves

filmiest open presses the wander if hills could world the costs

fluidity an essentially unbroken paths strung street too soon

8

dissolves the voyagers slant sunrise following the current

entered more us dissolves in a slow light you who are deepen

our memories in dim fold is full on distance which closes

our faces the same report the current door most the story

lost the boundary would fit a picture late from our footstep

the neither colourfully its operation with young more memoirist

of heart and subtle space begin dream through a saying

to die away sound the cast back ridge nearly and mouthed

in faithfulness torn from its wave becomes nor colour

winter coats own face perfect in cool water frame still

voyage an unseen window the icy days till splinter

9

heart push towards foam oh you so swift boarding

the little creatured dream through portholes memory

into the river in a story is a thing the loss comes an island

a farther moved by thinning which happens invisible

operations of water to die away hand every decked

wings are truths and run the straight of another voice

nor carry the forth mouth too kind by means of him

the motions of wandering the mirror first word

their operation wayward a last note as if lying for

with a clock in a room empty yet the chronological

dossiers a much larger passage unconnected with his end

in cool water that window the flowering of the dying begins

www.ingramcontent.com/pod-product-compliance
Lightning Source LLC
Chambersburg PA
CBHW051702040426
42446CB00009B/1255
9781912211661